W9-BWT-437

Flippers and Fins™

Swimming with

Manatees

Miriam Coleman

PowerKiDS
press™

New York

Published in 2010 by The Rosen Publishing Group, Inc.
29 East 21st Street, New York, NY 10010

First Edition

Editor: Joanne Randolph
Book Design: Greg Tucker
Photo Researcher: Jessica Gerweck

Photo Credits: Cover Daniel J. Cox/Getty Images; p. 5 © Kennan Ward/Corbis; p. 7 Brian Skerry/Getty Images; pp. 9, 21 Jeff Foott/Getty Images; pp. 11, 17 Paul Sutherland/Getty Images; p. 13 © Henno Robert/age fotostock; p. 15 Norbert Rosing/Getty Images; p. 19 © Daniel J. Cox/Corbis.

Library of Congress Cataloging-in-Publication Data

Coleman, Miriam.
  Swimming with manatees / Miriam Coleman. — 1st ed.
      p. cm. — (Flippers and fins)
  Includes index.
  ISBN 978-1-4042-8092-2 (library binding) — ISBN 978-1-4358-3241-1 (pbk.)
ISBN 978-1-4358-3242-8 (6-pack)
  1. Manatees—Juvenile literature. I. Title.
  QL737.S63C655 2010
  599.55—dc22
                                        2008051934

Manufactured in the United States of America

Contents

Meet the Sea Cow

A manatee moves slowly along the bottom of a river, **grazing** like a cow on the grass that grows on the riverbed. People sometimes call these peaceful animals sea cows.

Manatees are **marine mammals**. They have huge bodies covered in fat and thick, gray skin, which keep them warm in the water. Manatees spend their lives eating, resting, and traveling. They generally keep to themselves, but they gladly share their space with other manatees. They do not fight. When manatees get together in groups, they may even rub up against each other and play.

Manatees are friendly animals, but they do not really look for company. They are seen together in the same places because they are eating the same food.

How Many Manatees?

There are three different species, or types, of manatee. These are the West Indian manatee, the West African manatee, and the Amazonian manatee. Each species lives in a different part of the world, which you can tell from the species name.

You can tell the different species apart by the shape of their faces and heads, as well as their size. West Indian and West African manatees can grow to be 13 feet (4 m) long and can weigh up to 3,500 pounds (1,588 kg). The Amazonian manatee is the smallest of the three species. These manatees can grow to be 9 feet (3 m) long.

Manatees look like seals or walruses, but they are not related to them. The manatee's closest relatives are dugongs, elephants, and hyraxes.

Where Are the Manatees?

Manatees live only in warm water. They usually live in **shallow**, slow-moving water where lots of plants grow. You can find them swimming in rivers, bays, **estuaries**, and near coasts.

The Amazonian manatee lives in the Amazon and other rivers in South America. The West Indian manatee lives along coasts and in rivers between Brazil and the southeastern United States. Many of them live in Florida. The West African manatee lives near the western coast of Africa. Manatees migrate, which means that they move to new places to find food or warmer weather.

These two manatees swim in a shallow river in Florida. Manatees can live in salty water or freshwater.

Manatee Flippers

Manatees have two small flippers near their chests. Inside each flipper, the manatee has bones that are much like those in a person's arm and hand. Thick skin covers all the bones, making a shape like a paddle. The West African and West Indian manatees have three or four fingernails at the end of each flipper.

The flippers help manatees steer while they swim. In shallow water, manatees can use their flippers to walk along the ground. Manatees can also use their flippers to bring food to their mouths and to touch and scratch other manatees.

Here you can clearly see this manatee's flippers. You can see the nails on the flipper in this picture, too.

Finding Their Way in the Water

   Manatees have **sensitive whiskers** on their faces. The whiskers help manatees find food, even in muddy or dark waters. A manatee's skin is covered with other large, hard hairs. These hairs tell manatees how big other objects in the water are and how fast they are moving.

   Manatees also have very sensitive hearing. They can hear noises made both in the water and out of it. They can even tell where these noises come from. Manatees' ears are tiny holes behind their eyes. However, manatees actually take in the most sound through their large cheekbones.

The manatee's whiskers are so sensitive that each whisker connects to its own group of cells in the manatee's brain. Manatees also have good eyesight.

Veggie Lovers

Most manatees eat only vegetables, but they eat a lot of them. They eat different kinds of grass and leaves that they find growing in the water or at the water's edge.

To help break food into smaller pieces, manatees have bumpy pads on the roofs of their mouths. Manatees also have 24 to 32 teeth to chew up their food. The teeth wear down quickly because of the rough plants the manatees eat and the sand that gets mixed in with the plants. As one tooth gets worn down, another moves in to take its place.

A manatee can eat more than 100 pounds (45 kg) of plants in one day! It uses its long, movable upper lip to pull the food into its mouth.

Manatee Families

Manatees start their families late in life and grow their families slowly. A female manatee is ready to have a baby when she is five years old. Male manatees are not ready to become fathers until they are nine years old.

When manatees are ready to **breed**, they form groups called breeding herds. One female will swim with several males, sometimes for weeks. The males **compete** with each other to breed with the female.

When the female becomes pregnant, she carries the baby inside her for a year. Manatees have only one baby every two to five years.

If you see many manatees swimming together, you may be looking at a breeding herd. The males do not stay with the females once breeding is over.

Manatee Babies

Baby manatees are born underwater. As soon as they are born, they swim to the top to take a breath of air.

Newborn West Indian manatees are about 4 feet (1 m) long. They can weigh around 60 pounds (27 kg). Amazonian manatees are only about 30 inches (76 cm) long when they are born.

Baby manatees generally stay with their mothers for two years. The mothers nurse them for their first year. Baby manatees also start eating plants after a few weeks. The mothers teach the young manatees how to find food, where to rest, and where to migrate.

Here a manatee pup swims next to its mother. Manatees can live to be about 60 years old.

Manatees and People

American manatees have no known **predators** in nature. In the past, people hunted manatees for their meat, their skin, and the oil from their fat. Because manatees are so slow moving, they were easy to hunt.

Today many manatees are killed by mistake. When people come speeding by in motorboats, manatees cannot move out of the way, and they often get hit. Manatees can also drown when they get caught in fishing nets meant for other animals.

Manatee **habitats** are also in danger. People often pollute the waters where manatees live or drain rivers to build on the land.

Boat propellers kill many manatees. A propeller, like the one shown here, has blades that spin to make the boat move.

21

Save the Manatee

Manatees are an endangered species. This means that there are so few of them that they could become **extinct**. Because manatees breed slowly, it takes a long time to rebuild their **population** when some are killed. There are only about 3,000 manatees left in the United States.

Laws have been passed to save manatees. In the United States, it is **illegal** to hunt, kill, catch, or bother manatees. People who break this law must pay a fine and could even go to prison. Florida, where many manatees live, has set speed limits for boats in manatee habitats. The state has also made manatee **sanctuaries**, or places where manatees can live safely.

Glossary

breed (BREED) To make babies.

compete (kum-PEET) To try to get something that another animal wants.

estuaries (ES-choo-wer-eez) Areas of water where the ocean tides meet rivers.

extinct (ek-STINKT) No more of a certain kind alive.

grazing (GRAYZ-ing) Feeding on grass.

habitats (HA-beh-tats) The place where animals or plants naturally live.

illegal (ih-LEE-gul) Against the law.

marine mammals (muh-REEN MA-mulz) Warm-blooded animals that have backbones and hair, breathe air, feed milk to their young, and live in the water.

population (pop-yoo-LAY-shun) A group of animals or people living in the same area.

predators (PREH-duh-terz) Animals that kill other animals for food.

sanctuaries (SANK-choo-weh-reez) Safe places.

sensitive (SEN-sih-tiv) Can see or feel small differences.

shallow (SHA-loh) Not deep.

whiskers (HWIS-kerz) Hard hairs that grow on a face.

Index

Web Sites

Due to the changing nature of Internet links, PowerKids Press has developed an online list of Web sites related to the subject of this book. This site is updated regularly. Please use this link to access the list:

www.powerkidslinks.com/ffin/manatee/